THE
BAH
MEANS BUY
A HOUSE
PLAYBOOK

100 GOLDEN NUGGETS
FOR MILITARY WEALTH

QUICK, PUNCHY STRATEGIES
FOR FINANCIAL FREEDOM

ASK ANTWAUN

The BAH Means Buy A House Playbook

100 Golden Nuggets For Military Wealth

ISBN: 979-8-9936505-6-2

Published by AskAntwaun Media

All inquiries: AskAntwaun@gmail.com
Printed in the United States of America

Book Design by Williams DocuPrep
www.williamsdocuprep.com

Table of Contents

Acknowledgements

To every Soldier, Sailor, Airman, Marine, and guardian who serves this book is for you. You've sacrificed time, comfort, and certainty in service to your country. Now it's time to serve your future.

To my family, thank you for your patience, support, and belief when I worked late nights building this vision. And to every client, colleague, and mentor who shared their stories, your experiences shaped every page.

Service doesn't stop when you hang up the uniform. Sometimes, it just changes missions.

Introduction

Why This Playbook Exists

Most service members were never taught how money actually works. We learned how to ruck, how to qualify with a weapon, how to follow orders, and how to deploy on short notice. But nobody sat us down and said, "Hey, this is how you build wealth. This is how you use the benefits you earned. This is how you stop renting and start owning."

The truth? You can serve twenty years, earn a retirement, use your benefits responsibly, and still retire broke if you don't understand money.

I've seen too many good service members struggle, not because they're lazy or reckless, but because nobody ever taught them the rules of the financial game. And if you don't know the rules, you can't win. This playbook changes that.

This is not theory, not motivational fluff, and not

the same old "stop buying coffee" advice. This is a field manual of 100 Golden Nuggets, each one a clear, tactical move you can apply immediately. Every nugget is short on purpose. You don't need long speeches; you need clarity.

What you'll find in these pages are the real principles that built my wealth, helped my clients build theirs, and transformed the way military families use the benefits they already earned. You'll learn the moves I wish someone had taught me at 18, at 22, and at 30, before I missed opportunities I didn't even know existed.

You'll learn that:

- BAH is not "extra money"; it's leverage.

- VA loans aren't just home loans; they're a lifetime advantage.

- PCS moves aren't inconveniences; they're financial openings.

- Credit is not a trap; it's a tool when you know how to use it.

- Wealth is not luck; it's a system.

The goal of this book is simple. To give you 100 practical, proven, repeatable moves that shift your financial life forward. Some will challenge your thinking. Some will confirm what you felt but couldn't explain. And some will change the trajectory of your entire life.

Use the nuggets one at a time or all at once. Use them during a deployment, a PCS move, a career shift, or as you prepare for life after the uniform. Use them to build a life you don't need to escape from.

You serve your country. Now it's time to make your money serve you. Turn the page, and let's get to work.

Chapter 1

Mindset Nuggets (1–10)

*How You Think Determines
How You Build*

Nugget 1 — Your Paycheck Isn't Your Wealth

Most people confuse income with wealth. Your paycheck keeps you alive; your systems make you wealthy. If all your money does is pass through your hands, nothing changes. Wealth begins when your money stays in the family.

The Bottom Line

Wealth is not what you earn. It's what you keep, grow, and protect.

Nugget 2 — BAH Is Not "Extra Money" — It's Leverage

The biggest mindset shift in military finance: BAH is a government-paid investment deposit. You can either spend it on rent or turn it into ownership.

Same allowance. Different outcome. Rent disappears. Ownership compounds.

Nugget 3 — If You Don't Tell Your Money Where to Go, It Will Leave

Money behaves like a soldier without orders; it wanders. Your financial life needs command and control. Every dollar should have a job before it hits your account: save, invest, pay down, reinvest. If your money is not following orders, it's already out of formation.

Nugget 4 — Wealth Loves Structure

People think wealth comes from luck or timing. No, wealth comes from systems. Automatic payments. Automatic investments. Automatic savings. The wealthy aren't smarter. They automate smarter.

Nugget 5 — The Military Taught You Discipline. Use It.

You woke up early. You followed standards. You operated under pressure. Those same habits work even better with money. You don't need motivation, you need consistency. Financial discipline beats financial genius every time.

Nugget 6 — Ownership Is a Mindset Before It's a Status

Don't wait until you "feel ready" to buy a home, start a business, or invest. You become an owner the moment you start thinking like one. Owners plan differently. Owners spend differently. Owners expect returns, not excuses.

Nugget 7 — Every PCS Is an Opportunity, Not an Obstacle

Most service members see PCS as stress. Wealth builders see PCS as positioning. New market. New BAH rate. New investment angles. Every move gives you a chance people in the civilian world don't get.

Nugget 8 — Your Circle Determines Your Ceiling

If nobody around you talks about wealth, equity, or investments, your environment is capping your growth. Find your tribe lenders who educate you, real estate agents who know military strategy, mentors who think bigger. Your conversations will set your compensation.

Nugget 9 — Don't Chase Status. Chase Stability.

High car notes, luxury items, and lifestyle spending are wealth killers. The goal is not to look rich. The goal is to be free. Freedom > Flexing.

Nugget 10 — Wealth Is Boring Before It's Beautiful

The unsexy truth about building money: it looks boring for years. Slow growth. Consistent saving. Steady investing. Living slightly below your means. Then one day it's not boring anymore. You wake up with options.

The Bottom Line

Your mindset is the first filter through which your money flows. If the mindset is weak, every financial decision will be weak. But if the mindset is strong, structured, disciplined, and focused, wealth becomes inevitable. When you think differently, you move differently. When you move differently, you build differently.

Chapter 2

Money Management Nuggets (11–20)

Money Needs Orders. Give It a Chain of Command.

Nugget 11 — Budgeting Isn't Restriction. It's Intelligence.

A budget is not a punishment, it's a briefing. It tells you what's possible, what's waste, and what needs to change. People who refuse to budget aren't "free." They're flying blind. Money without intel becomes money lost.

Nugget 12 — Automate Everything You Can

If you depend on discipline alone, you'll lose. Set your bills, savings, and investments to autopilot. You don't rise to the level of your goals, you fall to the level of your systems. Remove human error. Make wealth automatic.

Nugget 13 — Track Cash Flow Like a Business, Not a Barracks Room

Your money has two jobs: come in and go out. If you don't track both, you'll always feel broke. Know your inflow. Know your outflow. Know your leftover. Clarity creates control.

Nugget 14 — Build a 3–6 Month Emergency Fund

Life happens. PCS delays, car repairs, medical surprises. If you don't prepare, crisis becomes debt. Start with $500, then $1,000, then a full 3–6 months. Security is not optional. It's the foundation.

Nugget 15 — Stop Leasing Your Lifestyle

Subscriptions, payment plans, high-interest cards. They're all ways of renting your life at full price. Buy what you need. Delay what you can. Own what matters.

Nugget 16 — Your First Raise Comes From Cutting Waste

Most people think they need more income. What they really need is less leakage.

Audit your last 90 days:

- Useless subscriptions
- Impulse food spending
- Convenience purchases
- Interest payments

Your next raise is already in your bank statements.

Nugget 17 — Build a Paycheck Battle Plan

Every payday, break your money into roles:

- Needs
- Goals
- Savings
- Investments
- Personal freedom spending

When every dollar has a job, you don't lose soldiers to friendly fire.

Nugget 18 — Treat Debt Like an Enemy, Not a Companion

Debt is not typical. It's a burden that drains your resources gradually and affects your future. Attack high-interest debt first. Never ignore it.

Consolidate when needed. Your mission is mobility, not bondage.

Nugget 19 — Keep Your Fixed Expenses Low

Your biggest financial risk is being "payment broke." If your rent, car notes, and bills eat your paycheck, you'll never get ahead even with a great salary. Flexibility is freedom. Lower your base load.

Nugget 20 — Make Saving a Requirement, Not a Reward

Most people save when they have extra. That means they never save. Treat savings like rent: non-negotiable, automated, and due every month. Pay your future self first.

The Bottom Line

Money management isn't about perfection. It's about predictability. When you give your money direction, it moves with purpose. When you remove emotion and rely on systems, progress becomes automatic. Money respects order. Give it a chain of command and watch it build wealth on autopilot.

Chapter 3

Credit & Leverage Nuggets (21–30)

Credit Isn't Dangerous. Ignorance Is.

Nugget 21 — Credit Is a Tool, Not a Trap

You've been told to fear credit. "No cards." "No loans." "No debt." But here's what nobody told you: Credit is the difference between struggling and scaling. Used well, it opens doors. Used poorly, it buries you. The strategy matters more than the card.

Nugget 22 — Your Credit Score Is a Report Card for Responsibility

Credit isn't emotional, it's math. It measures:

- On-time payments
- Credit usage
- Length of history
- Mix of accounts

- Recent activity

Strong credit lowers your interest, raises your buying power, and makes lenders compete for you. High score = low stress.

Nugget 23 — Never Use More Than 10–30% of Your Limit

This is the most misunderstood rule in credit. If your card has a $3,000 limit:

- 30% = $900
- 10% = $300

Staying under these ranges boosts your score fast. If you max your card out regularly, even if you pay it off your score drops. It's not about debt. It's about discipline.

Nugget 24 — Pay Your Card Twice a Month (the 15/3 Method)

This hack boosts your score without spending a dollar more.

Here's how:

- Pay once 15 days before the due date.
- Pay again 3 days before the due date.

This lowers reported utilization and raises your score because the bureaus see a lower balance. Small move. Big gain.

Nugget 25 — Don't Close Old Accounts

Your oldest accounts are gold. They extend your credit history and stabilize your score. Even if you don't use a card, keep it:

- Active
- At zero balance
- With one small recurring charge
- On auto-pay

Longevity equals trust.

Nugget 26 — Add Your Kids as Authorized Users (Legacy Credit Move)

You can start your child's credit before they graduate high school by adding them to your oldest, cleanest card.

It gives them:

- Instant credit history
- Lower interest rates later
- Faster approval for apartments or loans

This is how you break generational credit struggles.

Nugget 27 — Avoid Store Cards Like They're ALC at 4:59 p.m.

Store cards have:

- High interest
- Low limits
- High utilization impact
- Little long-term value

They're designed to trap you, not help you. If it doesn't build long-term leverage, skip it.

Nugget 28 — Know the Difference Between "Good Debt" and "Bad Debt"

Not all debt is the same.

Good debt:

- buys assets.
- increases value.
- produces income.
- lowers taxes.
- builds net worth.

Bad debt:

- buys liabilities.
- loses value immediately.
- charges high interest
- creates stress.

One brings freedom. One brings friction.

Nugget 29 — Credit Makes Real Estate Possible

Most people don't buy homes because of lack of cash. They don't buy because of lack of credit. Your credit score determines:

- Your rate
- Your monthly payment
- Your approval
- Your buying power
- Your options

VA loans forgive a lower score but great credit gives you flexibility.

Nugget 30 — Leverage Is the Wealth Multiplier

With the right credit, you can:

- Buy real estate with almost no money down.
- Access business funding

- Secure low-interest lines of credit.
- Move faster on opportunities.

Leverage is not about borrowing recklessly, it's about using credit strategically to grow faster than your income alone. This is how wealth accelerates.

The Bottom Line

Credit is the foundation of every major financial move you'll make. If you master it, doors open. If you ignore it, doors close. Treat your credit like a weapon. Clean it, sharpen it, and use it with precision.

Chapter 4

VA Loan Nuggets (31–40)

It's Not Just a Benefit. It's a Weapon.

Nugget 31 — Your VA Loan Is Not a One-Time Use

The biggest myth in the military is that it is. Truth is you can use your VA loan:

- More than once
- While owning another VA-financed home
- Even multiple times across different duty stations

Your entitlement resets when you sell or you can use remaining entitlement while keeping the first property. This benefit grows with you.

Nugget 32 — Entitlement Is Not a "Cap" — It's Capacity

Service members say, "My limit is $X." No. Your entitlement is the *amount the VA guarantees*, not your borrowing limit. There is no loan limit with full entitlement.

You can buy:

- $300K
- $600K
- $1.2M
- $2M+

The only limit is your income + the lender's approval. Stop thinking small.

Nugget 33 — You Can Own Multiple Properties With the VA

Example:

- Home #1 at previous duty station.
- PCS to new base.
- Use remaining entitlement for Home #2.
- Rent out Home #1.
- Build equity in both.

You don't need to "pay off the first" or "sell the first" to buy again. This is how service members build portfolios without realizing it.

Nugget 34 — VA Loans Don't Require a Down Payment, but They DO Require Discipline

No down payment doesn't mean "no skin in the game."

You still must:

- Budget properly.
- Avoid inflating your lifestyle.
- Keep cash reserves.
- Avoid blowing money on unnecessary furniture or cars.

Zero down is leverage but leverage requires control.

Nugget 35 — VA Funding Fee ≠ Closing Costs

The funding fee is a benefit cost, not a lender fee. It helps keep the program running. Here's the part people miss:

- It can be rolled into the loan.
- Many buyers don't pay it due to disability rating.
- You can still ask the seller to cover your closing costs separately.

Don't confuse the two.

Nugget 36 — Seller Credits Are Your Best Friend

With a VA loan, sellers can cover:

- Closing costs
- Temporary rate buydowns
- Permanent rate buydowns
- VA funding fee (if negotiated)
- Prepaids + escrows

This saves thousands and gets you in the home with little cash out of pocket. Savvy buyers negotiate. Uneducated buyers complain about prices.

Nugget 37 — Your BAH Is Already Paying Someone's Mortgage — Might as Well Be Yours

This is the nugget most service members ignore. Every month:

- BAH hits your account.
- You pay rent.
- Your landlord builds equity.

Switch the names: Your BAH → Your mortgage → Your equity, Same money. Different outcome. Completely different future.

Nugget 38 — The VA Loan Is the Lowest-Risk

Loan for Lenders

Truth: The VA loan has the lowest default rate of any major mortgage product. Why does that matter? Because it gives lenders confidence, which gives you better opportunities. Your loan is backed by the strongest guarantee in the country. Use it.

Nugget 39 — You Can Refinance Without Re-Qualifying (IRRRL)

The VA Interest Rate Reduction Refinance Loan (IRRRL) lets you:

- Lower your rate.
- Skip an appraisal.
- Skip income verification.
- Skip major underwriting.
- Roll in costs.

It's one of the most powerful tools in the VA system. Service members who don't use it leave thousands on the table.

Nugget 40 — The VA Assumption Is the Secret Weapon Almost No One Talks About

A VA assumable loan lets buyers:

- Take over your low interest rate.

- Keep your remaining years.
- Only pay the difference in equity.
- Potentially buy cheaper than market financing.

If you own a home with a low VA rate, you're sitting on a premium asset. If you're buying, it's the best deal in the entire housing market.

The Bottom Line

The VA loan is not a safety net; it's a launchpad. Most service members never learn how to maximize it.

Those who do build:

- Equity
- Cash flow
- Long-term security
- Generational advantage

You earned this benefit. Now it's time to use it like it was designed to create freedom.

Chapter 5

Real Estate Nuggets (41–50)

Property Isn't Just a Purchase. It's a Position.

Real estate is the bridge between your military income and your long-term wealth. Every door you buy becomes a new rank in your financial career. These 10 nuggets combine the smartest, most practical plays every military family can use without the fluff.

Nugget 41 — Demand Beats Prediction

You can't predict appreciation perfectly, nobody can. But you *can* predict demand:

- Military-stable markets.
- Tight inventory.
- Limited land.
- Strong population growth.

You're not betting on luck. You're betting on demand, and demand wins over time.

Nugget 42 — Equity Comes From More Than Appreciation

Equity has three engines, and you need all of them:

1. **Paydown** — every mortgage payment quietly raises your net worth.

2. **Buying right** — even a small discount accelerates returns.

3. **Appreciation** — icing on the cake.

Even when the market is flat, the first two are working behind the scenes.

Nugget 43 — Your First Home Is a Position, Not a Dream

Your first home doesn't need to be Instagram-worthy. It needs to be strategic.

Think:

- Affordable.
- Rentable.
- Resellable.

You're not committing forever. You're buying a stepping stone, and your future self will thank you.

Nugget 44 — Mission > Ego

Skip the ego buys. Skip the fancy upgrades. Skip the over-stretched budgets. Choose homes that match your mission:

- Strong comps
- Inspection solid
- Rent-ready
- Reasonable HOA

Luxury comes later. Strategy comes now.

Nugget 45 — House Hacking: The Military Wealth Shortcut

If you're single or dual-military, this is your cheat code. Live in one room → Rent the others → Let BAH + roommates pay down the mortgage. Simple. Legal. Powerful. Many service members hit six-figure net worth just from this move.

Nugget 46 — Multi-Units Build Wealth the Fastest

VA loans allow duplexes, triplexes, and fourplexes. That means:

- Live in one.

- Rent the rest.
- Mortgage covered.
- Cash flow possible.
- Appreciation multiplied.

This is one of the biggest missed opportunities in the entire military.

Nugget 47 — Location Is Really About the Exit Strategy

Forget zip code status. Ask these four questions instead:

- Will military families want to rent here?
- Do homes sell fast in this area?
- Are PCSing households constantly arriving?
- Will this property be assumable gold later?

The best location is the one with the best **exit**.

Nugget 48 — Renovations Don't Need to Be Fancy

High ROI improvements are simple:

- Paint
- Landscaping

- Fixtures
- Deep cleaning
- Basic kitchen/bath refreshes

Low cost. High impact. Maximum return. Save the big remodel dreams for your forever home, not your wealth-building home.

Nugget 49 — If You Don't Inspect It, You Don't Own It

Inspections protect you from:

- Roof problems.
- Foundation issues.
- Plumbing nightmares.
- Electrical hazards.
- Hidden water damage.

A $600 inspection can prevent a $20,000 mistake. This is not where you "save money."

Nugget 50 — Your Portfolio Is Built One Smart Move at a Time

Don't overthink it. Don't wait for the "perfect" time. Don't think you need $30K saved. One smart purchase → leveraged correctly → turns into three over a career. That's how military families build real portfolios.

The Bottom Line

Real estate isn't complicated; it's systematic. Follow these nuggets, stay disciplined, and leverage the military stability most people wish they had. Your real estate portfolio is not built in a day. It's built every time you choose strategy over emotion.

Chapter 6

Finance Nuggets (51–60)

*Your Money Should Move With a
Purpose, Not Vibes*

Most people don't have money problems. They have money management problems. When you give your dollars a mission, they follow orders. When you don't, they disappear. These nuggets are the financial discipline every military family should master—simple rules that keep your money tight, controlled, and working for you.

Nugget 51 — Every Dollar Needs a Job
Unassigned dollars get wasted. Assigned dollars get multiplied. Before the month starts, give every dollar purpose:

- Housing
- Savings
- Investing
- Bills

- Fun
- Future goals

If your money doesn't have orders, it goes AWOL.

Nugget 52 — Automate More Than You Trust Yourself To Do

Automation is discipline without effort. Automate:

- Savings
- Investments
- Bill payments
- Transfers
- Credit card payments

If it can be automated, automate it. You'll build wealth even on your busiest, most chaotic weeks.

Nugget 53 — A Budget Isn't Restriction — It's Freedom

A budget doesn't trap you. It gives you permission. When you know what's covered, you stress less and save more. Military analogy: A mission without logistics fails. Money without a plan does the same.

Nugget 54 — If You Don't Track It, You Can't Improve It

What gets measured gets mastered. Track:

- Income
- Expenses
- Debt balances
- Net worth

You don't need spreadsheets if that's not your thing. Use apps like:

- Mint
- YNAB
- Monarch
- Simplifi

If you don't know where your money is going, it's already gone.

Nugget 55 — Save First, Spend Second

Most people save what's left. Wealthy people save *before* money leaves. Set your savings to auto-pull on payday. If you never see it, you never miss it. This one move alone turns undisciplined spenders into consistent builders.

Nugget 56 — Emergency Funds Create Confidence, Not Fear

An emergency fund is not optional. It's your buffer between inconvenience and disaster.

Goal: Three to six months of living expenses. If that's too big, start with:

- $500
- Then $1,000
- Then one month

Stack small wins until you build the full wall.

Nugget 57 — Stop Financing Your Lifestyle With Debt

High-interest debt steals future income. If you're paying:

- 20% interest on credit cards
- 15% on personal loans
- 25% on car loans

You're not living; you're renting your lifestyle from the bank.

Use debt only for:

- Real estate

- Business
- Strategic leverage

Not for everyday spending.

Nugget 58 — Your Car Payment Should Never Compete With Your Mortgage

The #1 wealth killer in the military? Car payments. People drive their wealth instead of building it. Rule of thumb: If your car payment is close to your mortgage…your priorities are backwards. Buy reliable. Not status.

Nugget 59 — The 70/20/10 Rule for Financial Peace

A simple breakdown that works for most families:

- **70%** — Living expenses
- **20%** — Savings & investments
- **10%** — Giving or future projects

Adjust the percentages, but never the principle: Purpose > randomness.

Nugget 60 — Increase Income Before You Increase Lifestyle

Lifestyle creep is the silent thief of wealth. Every time you get:

- A pay raise.
- BAH increase.
- Bonus.
- Tax refund.

Give at least half to savings, investing, or debt payoff before you upgrade anything. Your future self will thank you.

The Bottom Line

Money doesn't respond to hope. It responds to action, structure, and discipline—the same things the military trained you for. Master these financial nuggets, and the next chapters will accelerate everything you're building.

Chapter 7

Military Advantage Nuggets (61–70)

The Military Gives You Tools Most Americans Will Never Have — Use Them

Service members walk around with wealth-building advantages hidden in plain sight. Most never use them. Some don't even know they exist. These nuggets break down the financial benefits only military members get and how to weaponize them.

Nugget 61 — BAH Is a Wealth Engine, Not "Free Rent Money"

BAH was never meant to be spent. It was meant to be leveraged. When you use BAH to:

- Buy a home.
- Build equity.
- Cover rental property expenses.

- House hack

You turn a benefit into a portfolio. When you use it to rent, it disappears forever.

Nugget 62 — COLA Is Not a Raise — It's an Opportunity

COLA comes and goes. But what you do with it leaves a lasting impact. Use COLA to:

- Increase savings.
- Boost investing.
- Catch up on emergency funds.
- Cover PCS-related expenses without using credit.

Most people treat it like bonus money. Winners treat it like a financial accelerator.

Nugget 63 — The GI Bill Isn't Just for School — It's a Family Wealth Transfer Tool

The GI Bill can:

- Fund your education.
- Cover your spouse's degree.
- Pay for your child's schooling.

Or the big play: Use your GI Bill for *YOU*, then use VA loan leverage and military income to build assets your kids inherit. Education + assets = generational advantage.

Nugget 64 — The TSP Match Is Free Money — Don't Leave It on the Table

DoD matches up to 5%. If you're not getting the full match, you're rejecting part of your paycheck. Think of TSP matching as a guaranteed 100% return on your contribution. Nothing in civilian investing comes close.

Nugget 65 — Deployments Come With Financial Buffers Most Families Never Get

Deployment =

- Extra pay.
- Tax-free income.
- Reduced spending.
- Savings spike.
- Loan interest freeze (for some pay grades).

Most see deployments as strain. But financially?

They're a launch pad if you plan correctly. Use deployment income to:

- Pay off debt.
- Build emergency savings.
- Invest heavily.
- Stack your down payment or assumption gap.

A year of discipline can set up a decade of peace.

Nugget 66 — Bonuses Aren't Spending Money — They're Leverage

Reenlistment bonuses and retention incentives can be:

- Seed money for a rental property
- Down payment savings
- Debt elimination
- Business startup capital
- Investment lump-sum boosts

Blow a bonus once = Gone. Invest a bonus once = Permanent.

Nugget 67 — VA Disability Isn't Just Compensation — It's a Financial Advantage

It's tax-free income. It's stability after service. It increases loan qualification. It's potential property tax exemptions depending on your state.

Disability pay can unlock:

- Lower DTI (Debt-to-Income Ratio)
- Higher purchase power
- Stronger long-term financial stability

It's not charity. It's earned benefit, use it.

Nugget 68 — Military Travel Gives You Micro-Investing Opportunities Everywhere You Go

Every PCS, TDY, or assignment exposes you to:

- New markets
- Different cost of living
- Job opportunities
- Real estate variations

Track:

- Rent prices.
- Home values.
- Appreciation trends.

- Industry growth.

You don't have to invest everywhere, but awareness alone is a competitive edge.

Nugget 69 — Military Networks Are the Ultimate Business & Wealth Pipeline

The military community is:

- Loyal.
- Trust-based.
- Word-of-mouth driven.

Whether it is:

- Real estate.
- Entrepreneurship.
- Skilled trades.
- Services.
- Partnerships.

Your network is your net worth especially in the military, where reputation is currency.

Nugget 70 — Your Service Gives You Access to Wealth Most People Will Never See

The military gives you:

- Low-cost healthcare
- Housing benefits
- Education opportunities
- Retirement options
- Job stability

When combined with discipline, these benefits become a powerful wealth engine. The world loves to say, "military pay is low." But military opportunity is unmatched.

The Bottom Line

Your service comes with built-in financial advantages that civilians dream about. When you stack them correctly housing, education, income stability, retirement tools, and tax benefits you create a wealth system that grows long after you hang up the uniform. You earned these benefits. Now it's time to utilize them.

Chapter 8

Entrepreneurship Nuggets (71–80)

You Don't Need Permission To Build Wealth — Just Initiative

Entrepreneurship isn't a mystery. It's a skill set, and military members already have the core skills: discipline, systems, leadership, problem-solving, and execution under pressure.

These nuggets show you how to turn what you already know into income, ownership, and long-term wealth.

Nugget 71 — Your Military Skills Are Monetizable

Everything you learned in service translates into value:

- Military skill → Civilian value
- Training → Consulting
- Leadership → Management or coaching
- Maintenance/logistics → High-demand trades
- Security → Contracting
- Planning → Operations work

You already have the raw materials for business. Entrepreneurship is just packaging what you know.

Nugget 72 — Start Small, Start Lean, Start Now

You don't need:

- A fancy brand
- A website
- A big loan
- A 20-page business plan

What you need:

- A skill
- A customer
- Consistency

Start with one client→ Improve→ Repeat→ Scale. Everything else is noise.

Nugget 73 — Your First Business Doesn't Need To Be Your Last

Your first business is your training ground. It might be:

- A cleaning service
- A coaching gig
- A repair business
- Photography
- Amazon reselling
- Real estate services

It doesn't have to be perfect. It just has to move. Your first business teaches you the game. Your second one makes money. Your third changes your family.

Nugget 74 — Solve a Problem, Don't Sell a Product

Military members pay for:

- Reliability
- Clarity
- Speed
- Solutions

Not just "stuff." Ask yourself: "What problem am I solving that people actually care about?" If the answer is strong, money will follow.

Nugget 75 — Use the GI Bill as Your Business Incubator

Nobody talks about this — but they should. Your GI Bill can act like:

- Free education
- A paid apprentice program
- A certification fund
- Skill acquisition training
- A launchpad into higher-demand fields

You literally get PAID to learn. That is entrepreneurship fuel.

Nugget 76 — Don't Fear Competition — Fear Being Invisible

There are thousands of people doing what you want to do. That's good. That means:

- There's demand.
- There's a proven market.
- People pay for your service.

Your job isn't to be the only one. Your job is to be the trusted one.

Nugget 77 — A Simple System Beats a Complex Vision Every Time

The most successful veteran entrepreneurs don't run complicated operations. They run *repeatable systems*. Your system could be:

- 3 steps to onboard a client.
- 2 tools to manage your calendar and invoicing.
- 1 weekly review.
- 1 monthly strategy update.

Simplicity scales. Complexity kills momentum.

Nugget 78 — Social Media Is Free Marketing — Use It With Discipline

You don't need to go viral. You just need to show up consistently.

Post:

- What you do
- Who you help

- Your knowledge
- Your results
- Your personality

You're not posting for strangers. You're posting for the people already watching. Visibility = opportunity.

Nugget 79 — Don't Quit Your Job — Replace Your Job

Your goal is not to "take a leap of faith." Your goal is to build a bridge.

Steps:

1. Start a business part-time.
2. Build steady revenue.
3. Cover your expenses.
4. THEN leave.

Leaving too early kills dreams. Leaving too late kills progress. Leaving at the right time builds legacy.

Nugget 80 — Entrepreneurship Is Ownership — Ownership Is Freedom

The military gave you structure. Entrepreneurship gives you choice. When you build a business, you're not just creating income; you're creating:

- Equity
- Autonomy
- Time freedom
- Legacy pathways
- Options for your family

Ownership is the highest rank in wealth.

The Bottom Line

Entrepreneurship isn't for "special" people. It's for disciplined people. And nobody is more disciplined than the military. You already know how to plan, adapt, and execute. Now apply those same tools to building your income, your independence, and your family's future.

Chapter 9

Family Legacy Nuggets (81–90)

Wealth Isn't What You Leave Them.
It's What You Teach Them.

Most families think legacy is money. But real legacy is mindset, systems, and structure—the things that keep the money growing long after you're gone. These nuggets show you how to build a legacy that lasts more than a lifetime.

Nugget 81 — Legacy Starts With Vision, Not Money

Every family needs a mission statement. Something like: *"We build wealth, we protect wealth, and we use it to help the next generation advance."* If your family doesn't know the mission, they won't understand the decisions you're making today. Write it. Share it. Live it.

Nugget 82 — Teach Values Before You Teach Numbers

Kids who understand:

- Discipline
- Gratitude
- Delayed gratification
- Responsibility

...become adults who handle money well. Teach them *why* before you teach them *how*. Character protects wealth better than any trust.

Nugget 83 — Run Your Home Like a Team, Not a Secret Society

The "don't talk about money" mindset keeps families broke. Instead:

- Let your kids see you budget.
- Explain why you chose the house you bought.
- Talk openly about goals.
- Hold family financial briefings.

You're not oversharing, you're training future leaders.

Nugget 84 — Create Income That Survives You

Wages stop when you stop. Assets don't. Focus on building:

- Cash-flowing real estate.
- Long-term rental equity.
- Index fund portfolios.
- A family business.
- Dividends and royalties.

Your goal is *intergenerational momentum*, not just savings.

Nugget 85 — Every Family Needs a Legacy Folder

This is not optional. Your legacy folder should include:

- Will or trust.
- Life insurance details.
- Account access information.
- Property records.
- Business documents.
- Passwords.
- Monthly expenses.

- Emergency instructions.

If something happens to you, your family should be able to move forward without chaos.

Nugget 86 — A Trust Isn't Only for the Wealthy — It's for the Wise

A living trust helps you:

- Avoid probate.
- Transfer assets cleanly.
- Protect children.
- Control how money is used.
- Guard your legacy from mismanagement.

Your next generation deserves order, not legal confusion.

Nugget 87 — Teach the Next Generation How To Make Money, Not Just Save It

Saving is safe. But earning is power. Teach your kids:

- How to spot opportunities.
- How to solve problems.
- How to start something small.

- How to use skills to create value.

Their confidence will be worth more than anything you leave behind.

Nugget 88 — Don't Just Build Wealth — Explain It

Tell your kids:

- How you bought your first house.
- How you fixed your credit.
- How you invested.
- What mistakes you made.
- What you learned.

Your story is strategy. Your transparency is their blueprint.

Nugget 89 — Make Legacy a Lifestyle, Not a Lecture

Legacy isn't a speech, it's:

- What you model
- What you prioritize
- What you discuss
- What you celebrate

Kids copy what you do, not what you preach. Live the lesson.

Nugget 90 — Your Legacy Is Built Daily, Not Someday

Small daily habits matter more than one big event. Every time you:

- Save.
- Invest.
- Teach.
- Budget.
- Plan.
- Communicate.

...you're laying bricks your grandchildren will walk on. Legacy is built through consistency, not complexity.

The Bottom Line

Your family doesn't need perfection, they need preparation. You're not just leaving wealth behind... you're leaving a playbook. Build the habits. Teach the principles and pass the mission.

Chapter 10

The Final 10 Nuggets (91–100)

*Ask Antwaun Law – The Wealth
Laws I Live By*

These aren't tips or theories. These are the laws, the rules that guided my journey and the principles behind every book in this series. Live by these, and you'll build wealth even if you never memorize another chapter.

Nugget 91 — BAH Is Not a Benefit. It's a Building Tool.

If you spend your BAH, it's gone. If you leverage it, it becomes equity, rent checks, and long-term security. BAH is the military's built-in wealth machine; use it.

Nugget 92 — Your First Goal Isn't Owning a Home. It's Owning an Asset.

Your first purchase should work for you:

- Rents easily.
- Sells easily.
- Assumes easily.
- Appreciates steadily.

If it doesn't help build your future, it doesn't belong in your portfolio.

Nugget 93 — Credit Is a Weapon. Protect It. Deploy It. Never Misfire.

Good credit:

- Lowers your cost of money.
- Opens doors.
- Gives leverage instead of limitations.

Guard it like rank. Use it like strategy.

Nugget 94 — Never Move for the Military Without Moving for Your Money Too.

Every PCS is a business opportunity disguised as orders.

- New BAH.
- New market.

- New leverage.

If you treat PCSing like relocation instead of ele-vation, you leave your wealth on the tarmac.

Nugget 95 — Your VA Loan Is a Lifetime Tool — Not a One-Time Ticket.

- Use it.
- Reuse it.
- Stack it.
- Assume it.
- Leverage it.
- Build with it.

The only people who don't benefit from the VA loan are the ones who never learned to play the game.

Nugget 96 — Wealth Isn't Fast. But It Is Predictable.

If you:

- Buy smart.
- Invest consistently.
- Reuse benefits.

- Protect credit.
- Stay disciplined.

...wealth becomes math, not magic.

Nugget 97 — Your Money Should Always Have a Mission.

Every dollar should be assigned:

- Build
- Protect
- Grow
- Pay down
- Position

Unassigned money gets wasted. Assigned money gets multiplied.

Nugget 98 — Ownership Beats Opportunity. Always.

Renters get options. Owners get outcomes. If you own assets, you control the game. If you don't, the game controls you.

Nugget 99 — Wealth Without Systems Will

Collapse.

Systems build consistency. Consistency builds results. Results build legacy.

- Budget.
- Automate.
- Review.
- Reinvest.
- Repeat.

This is how wealth survives generations.

Nugget 100 — Freedom Comes From Discipline, Not Desire.

Everyone wants wealth. Few are disciplined enough to build it. Your habits are the difference:

- Showing up
- Saving first
- Investing consistently
- Planning ahead
- Moving strategically
- Using benefits wisely

Discipline creates the freedom everyone else wishes for.

The Bottom Line

You don't need luck. You need structure. You need intention. You need these laws. Apply them daily and you'll build wealth your kids and their kids will thank you for.

Epilogue

The Last Formation

By now, you've seen the pattern: Wealth isn't luck. It isn't a secret. It isn't something "other people" build. It's structure. It's decisions. It's discipline. It's the same discipline you've lived your entire military career. Everything in this book, every nugget, is meant to do one thing: shift you from reacting to money… to commanding it.

Because the truth is simple: Most people let life happen to them. Service members don't. We plan. We prepare. We execute. And when we carry those same habits into our finances, we build something bigger than any paycheck can measure.

Here's the part nobody tells you: You don't need the perfect job. You don't need the perfect market. You don't need the perfect timing. You just need the right systems, used consistently.

If you take these 100 nuggets and apply even half

of them, your entire financial trajectory changes not eventually, but immediately.

And when you start stacking wins month after month, PCS after PCS, assignment after assignment... you look up one day and realize that you've built something permanent.

This isn't the end of the journey. It's the moment you stop waiting and start leading your financial life with intent. The mission from here is simple:

1. Build your wealth.

2. Protect your wealth.

3. Teach your wealth.

4. Pass on your wealth.

Your service earned you benefits most people never get. Your discipline gives you an advantage most people never use. Your actions from here determine whether your family remembers your rank... or your legacy. You're ready. Now move with purpose.

About The Author

Antwaun Hill is a U.S. Army veteran, real estate professional, and educator based in Hawaii. After 13 years of active-duty service, he transitioned to civilian life and discovered how misunderstood military financial benefits truly were, including his own.

That realization sparked a mission: to help service members, veterans, and military families use the VA loan, BAH, and PCS opportunities to build lasting wealth. As the founder of **Ask Antwaun**, he's become a trusted voice for military real estate education, blending strategy, storytelling, and empowerment.

Through his brand and book series, *BAH Means Buy A House*, Antwaun continues to teach one core message: "You already have the benefits. You just need to learn how to use them."

Follow him on Instagram **@AskAntwaun**

Contact: **AskAntwaun@gmail.com**

Other books in this series